EXTREME SCIENCE

POWERFUL FORCES

Rob Colson and Jon Richards

Gareth Stevens
PUBLISHING

I0811055

Please visit our website, www.garethstevens.com. For a free color catalog of all our high-quality books, call toll free 1-800-542-2595 or fax 1-877-542-2596.

Cataloging-in-Publication Data

Names: Colson, Rob. | Richards, Jon.
Title: Powerful forces / by Rob Colson and Jon Richards.
Description: New York : Gareth Stevens Publishing, 2024. | Series: Extreme science | Includes glossary and index.
Identifiers: ISBN 9781538288870 (pbk.) | ISBN 9781538288887 (library bound) | ISBN 9781538288894 (ebook)
Subjects: LCSH: Force and energy--Juvenile literature. | Motion--Juvenile literature.
Classification: LCC QC73.4 C563 2024 | DDC 531'.6--dc23

Published in 2024 by
Gareth Stevens Publishing
2544 Clinton St.
Buffalo, NY 14224

Editor: Amy Pimperton
Text written by Rob Colson and Jon Richards
Produced by Tall Tree Ltd
Designers: Malcolm Parchment and Ben Ruocco

Picture credits:
Every attempt has been made to clear copyright. Should there be any inadvertant omission, please apply to the publisher for rectification.

First published in Great Britain in 2019 by Wayland Copyright © Hodder and Stoughton, 2019

All rights reserved. No part of this book may be reproduced in any form without permission in writing from the publisher, except by a reviewer.

Printed in the United States of America

CPSIA compliance information: Batch #CSGS24: For further information contact Gareth Stevens at 1-800-542-2595.

Find us on

CONTENTS

WHAT ARE FORCES?

Forces are pushes and pulls that act on objects, affecting how they behave. Forces can be big or small and they can act over tiny distances or across the entire universe.

FOUR FUNDAMENTAL FORCES

Scientists talk about four fundamental forces at work in the universe.

1 Gravity attracts objects that have mass. It keeps planets orbiting stars and pulls objects on Earth toward the ground.

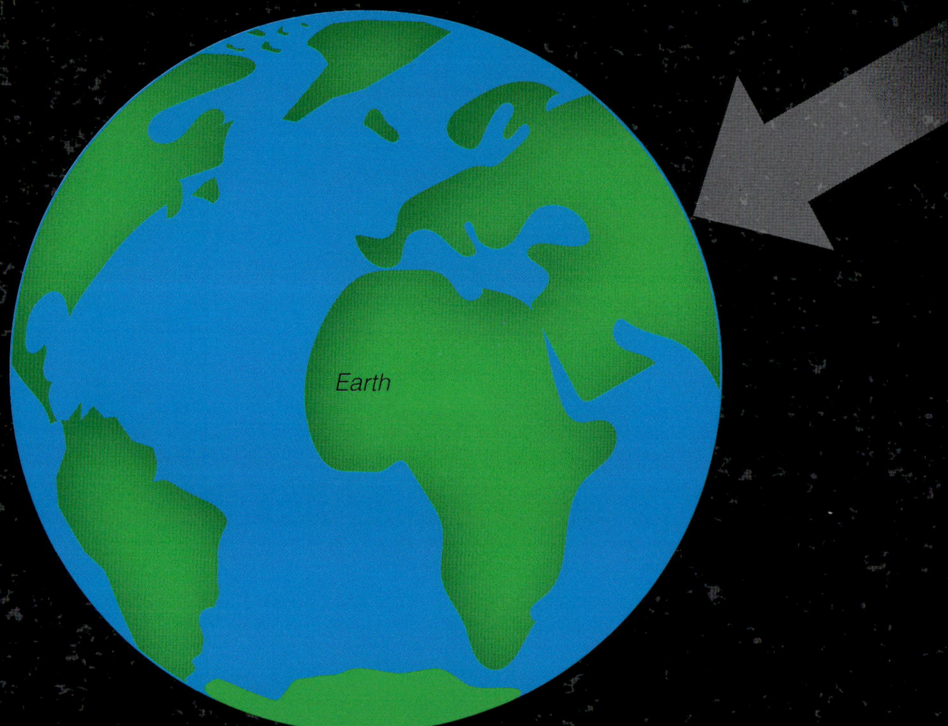

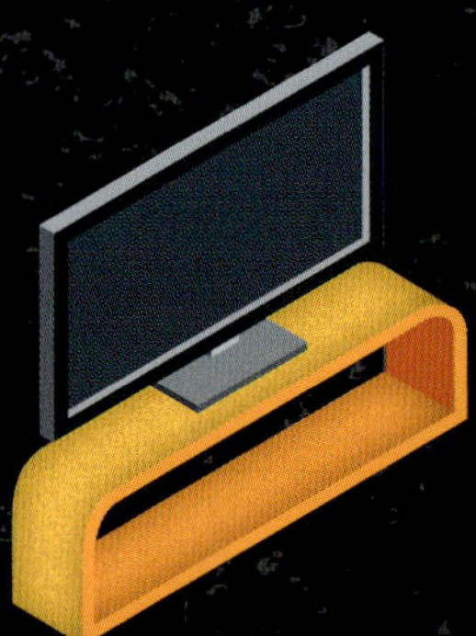

2 Electromagnetism holds the atoms of objects together. Electromagnetic interactions produce light, such as the pictures on a TV screen.

3 Weak nuclear force is responsible for radioactive decay and plays an important role in nuclear fusion that powers stars, such as the sun.

4 Strong nuclear force holds an atom's nucleus together. This energy is released when atoms are split, as in an atomic explosion.

Gravity keeps Earth in orbit around the sun.

FORCES IN ACTION

You might not be able to actually see forces, but you can detect their effects.

GRAVITY is pulling this jet down to the ground. The shape of the aircraft produces a force called **LIFT**, which acts against gravity to keep the jet in the air. Where lift and gravity are equal, the aircraft maintains a constant height.

THRUST produced by the engines pushes the plane forward.
DRAG produced by the jet moving through the air acts against the plane's movement. Where drag and thrust are equal, the aircraft maintains a constant speed.

ACTING TOGETHER

Forces usually do not act on their own and there may be two or more forces acting on an object.

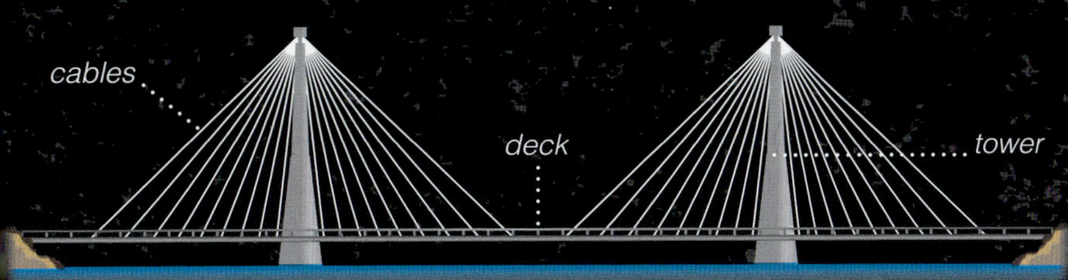

Balanced forces
This bridge doesn't fall down because the weight of its deck equals the supporting forces of the towers and cables.

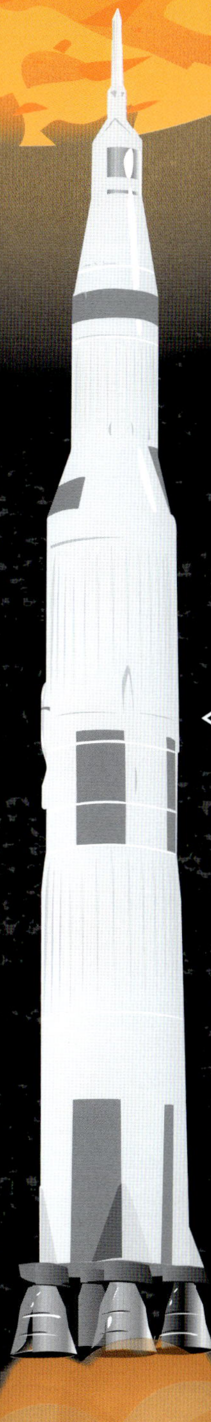

Unbalanced forces
The upward thrust produced by this rocket's engines is greater than the force of gravity pulling it down, so it can blast off.

EXTREME GRAVITY

Gravity is a force that attracts all objects with mass, which is the amount of physical matter something has. Objects that have a lot of mass, such as planets and stars, will have a lot of gravity, while objects with little mass, including you, will only have small amounts of gravitational force.

APPLES AND TREES

Everything around you is affected by gravity, from a small apple in your hand to a towering tree. Earth's gravity attracts objects toward its center. When you throw an apple in the air, or if you cut down the tree, they will both fall to the ground. At the same time, Earth will also be attracted to them (but only by a tiny amount).

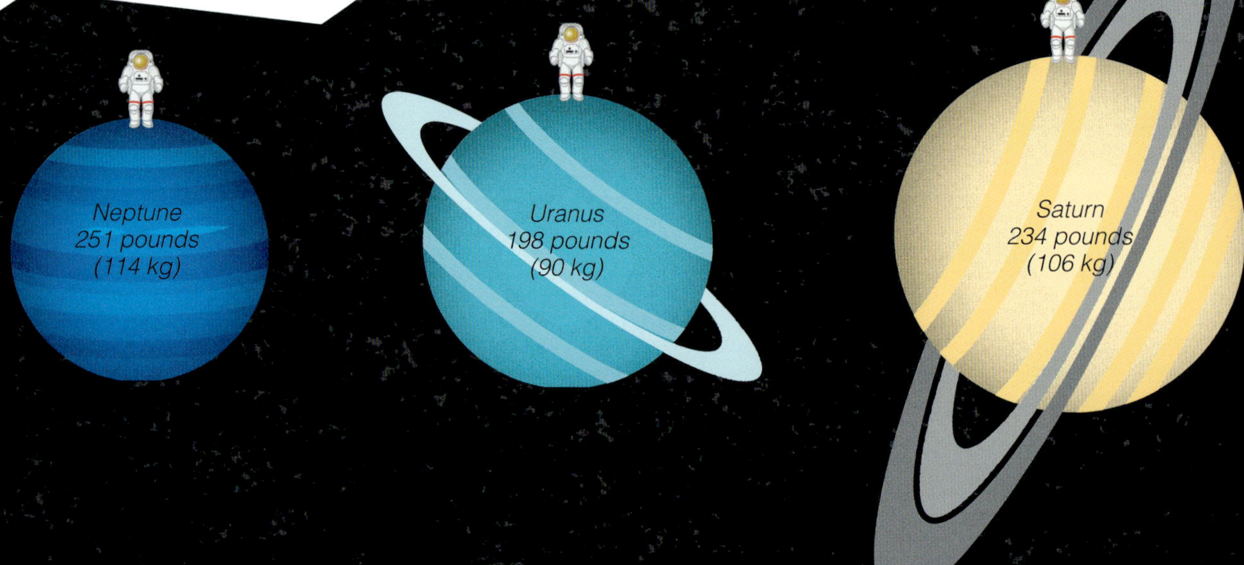

HOLDING THE UNIVERSE TOGETHER

The effects of gravity are felt right across the universe. Stars are attracted to each other in their billions to form huge star cities, or galaxies. These galaxies are also attracted to each other to form clusters. Extreme superclusters are some of the biggest structures in the universe, containing millions and millions of galaxies.

SHINING STARS

Deep in the heart of stars, the immense force of gravity squeezes atomic nuclei together until they fuse. This fusion releases huge amounts of energy as light and heat, causing the stars, including our sun, to shine.

GRAVITY AND WEIGHT

The stronger the force of gravity, the greater an object's weight. If you traveled to all of the planets in the solar system, your weight would be different on each one. You would be heaviest on Jupiter because the surface of Jupiter experiences the strongest gravitational pull.

FASTER AND FASTER

If you add more force to a moving object in its direction of movement, its speed will increase. This is known as acceleration and it can have interesting effects on us humans.

ACCELERATION ON EARTH

The acceleration caused by Earth's gravity is 9.8 meters per second per second (**ms^2**). This is often referred to as **g**.

Negative g is an extreme force causing a body to accelerate downward faster than the rate of natural free fall.

-3 g (negative 3 g) is the limit of negative g before a human "reds out." This is when blood is pushed up into the head, which can damage vision and even cause a stroke. Fighter pilots can experience -3 g.

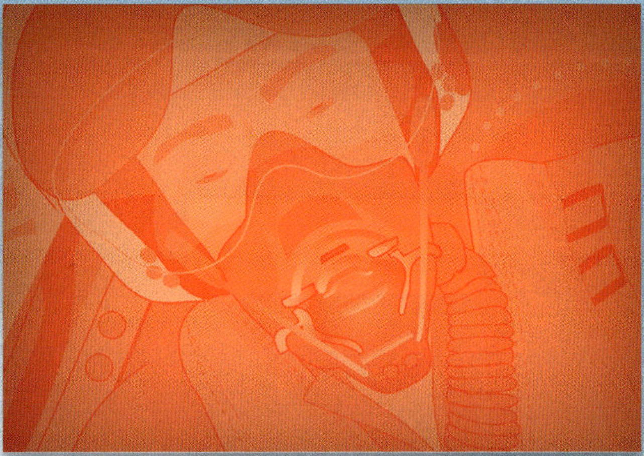

standing on Earth at sea level; what we experience every day:
1 g

standing on the moon:
0.1654 g

Earth and moon (not to scale)

5 g is the usual human tolerance before blacking out.

upper limit handled by modern pilots:
9 g

maximum experienced by a human on a rocket sled:
42.6 g

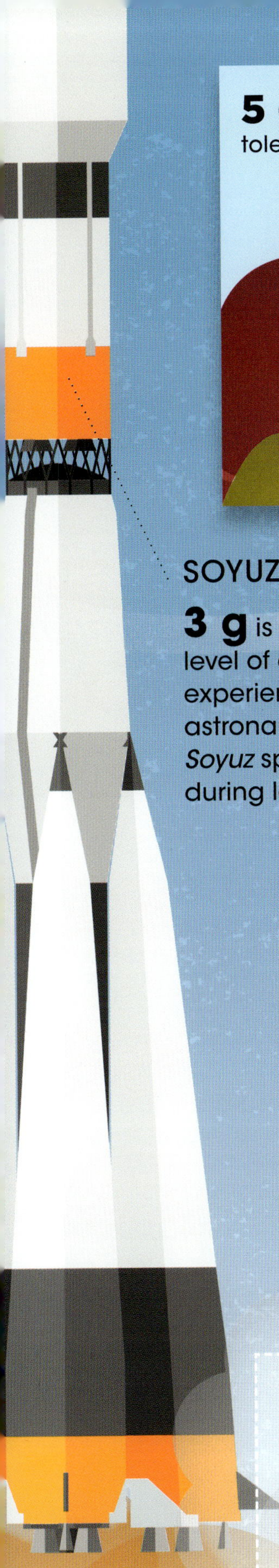

SOYUZ

3 g is the greatest level of acceleration experienced by astronauts on the *Soyuz* spacecraft during launch.

214 g
is the highest recorded g survived by a human, Kenny Bräck, who crashed during an Indycar race in Texas.

tolerance of electronics in modern artillery shells:
15,500 g

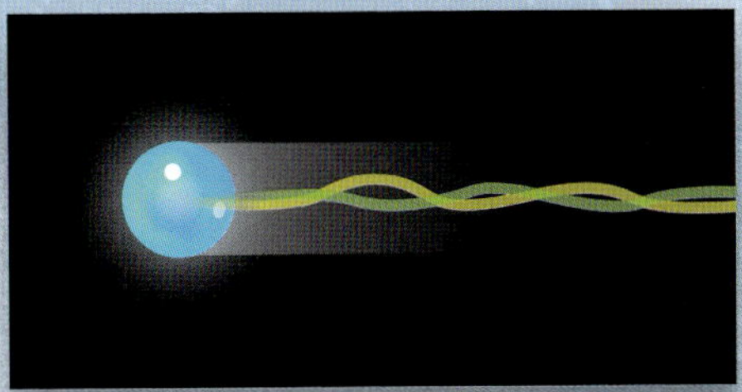

acceleration of a proton in the Large Hadron Collider particle accelerator:
190,000,000 g

Scientists have subjected some species of **bacteria** to forces in excess of
400,000 g.
Using an **ultracentrifuge**, they spun the bacteria around very quickly and found that they still grew!

COMING TO A STOP

Getting faster and faster is all well and good, but sometimes you just want to stop. Like acceleration, deceleration (or "negative acceleration" as some scientists call it) needs a force to change how the object is moving.

STOPPING A RACING CAR

- A Formula 1 car's brakes can decelerate it from about 60 miles (100 km) per hour to 0 in just 50 feet (15 m).
- In comparison, a normal high-performance car needs about 100 feet (31 m)—about twice as much. It is heavier than a Formula 1 car, so it needs more force to slow it down.

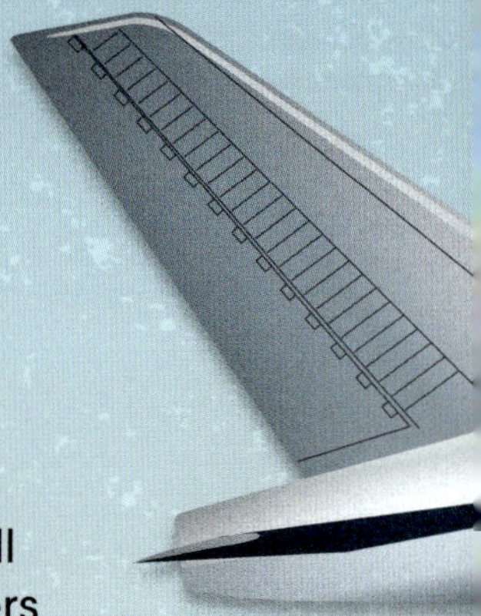

OIL TANKERS

Even with their engines in full reverse, the largest oil tankers are so heavy that they need as much as 5 miles (8 km) to come to a complete stop.

AIRCRAFT CARRIERS

Aircraft carriers have very short flight decks to land on. To bring aircraft to a halt quickly, they are fitted with strong arrestor wires that are caught by a tailhook on the back of the aircraft to stop it.

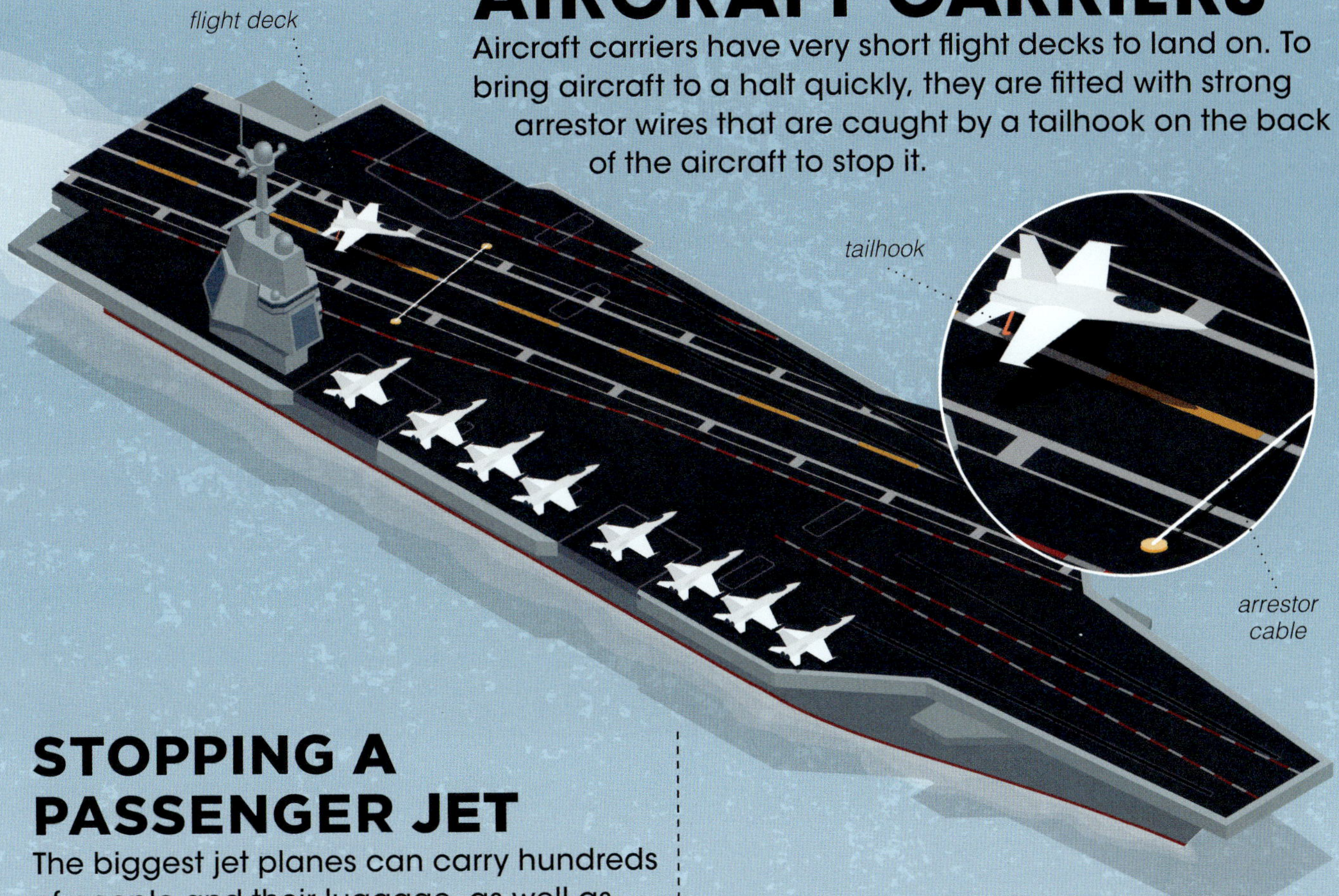

STOPPING A PASSENGER JET

The biggest jet planes can carry hundreds of people and their luggage, as well as heavy jet engines, fuel and equipment. When they come in to land at hundreds of miles an hour, they need several systems to bring them to a halt.

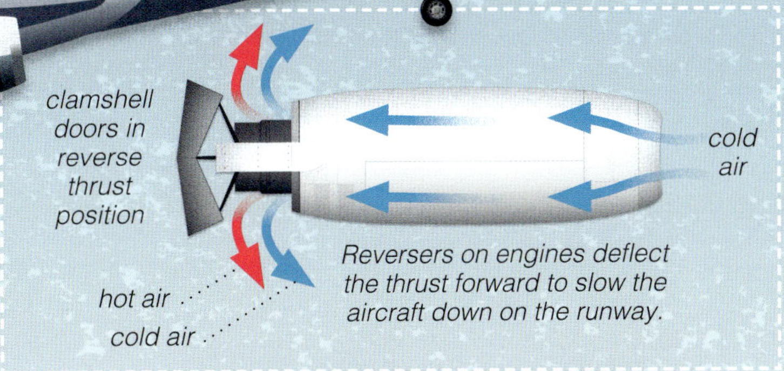

THRUSTING FORWARD

Push against something and it will push back—this simple fact can be very helpful if you need to blast along at high speeds or lift super-heavy weights.

HOW THRUST WORKS

British scientist Sir Isaac Newton (1642–1727) explained that "for every action, there is an equal and opposite reaction." This means that when something pushes against something else, it receives an equal force in return. So when a jet engine creates a blast of hot gases that pushes out backward, it creates the thrust to push the jet forward.

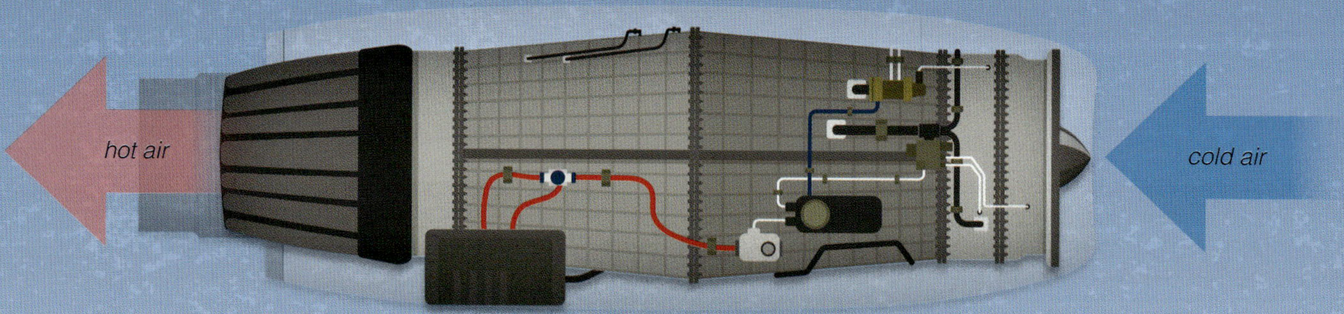

A fan at the front of the engine sucks in large quantities of air. The air is squeezed and mixed with fuel. The fuel and air mixture catches fire, reaching temperatures of more than 1,832°F (1,000°C). This creates hot air that leaves the back of the engine at high speed, pushing the aircraft forward.

F-35 Lightning II: **191.3 kN**

EXTREME THRUST

A Newton (N) is the unit used to measure force. 1 kN (kilonewton) = 1,000 Newtons.

F-15 Eagle: **133.4 kN**

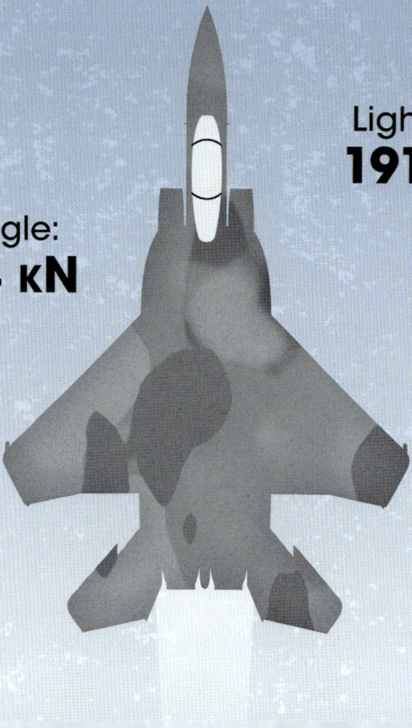

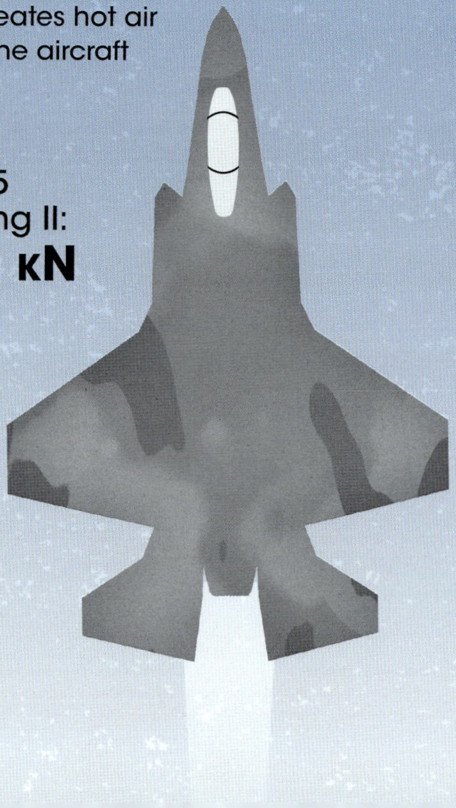

The force produced by a firearm is called bolt thrust. When someone fires a rifle, they need to brace their body to absorb the force pushing back at them, which is equal and opposite to the bolt thrust.

a **.22 caliber** rifle cartridge on firing: **4 kN** of thrust.

Extreme thrust needs lots of fuel. During lift-off, **Saturn V** burned **16.5 tons (15 mt)** of fuel per second.

X-15 hypersonic aircraft: **250 kN**

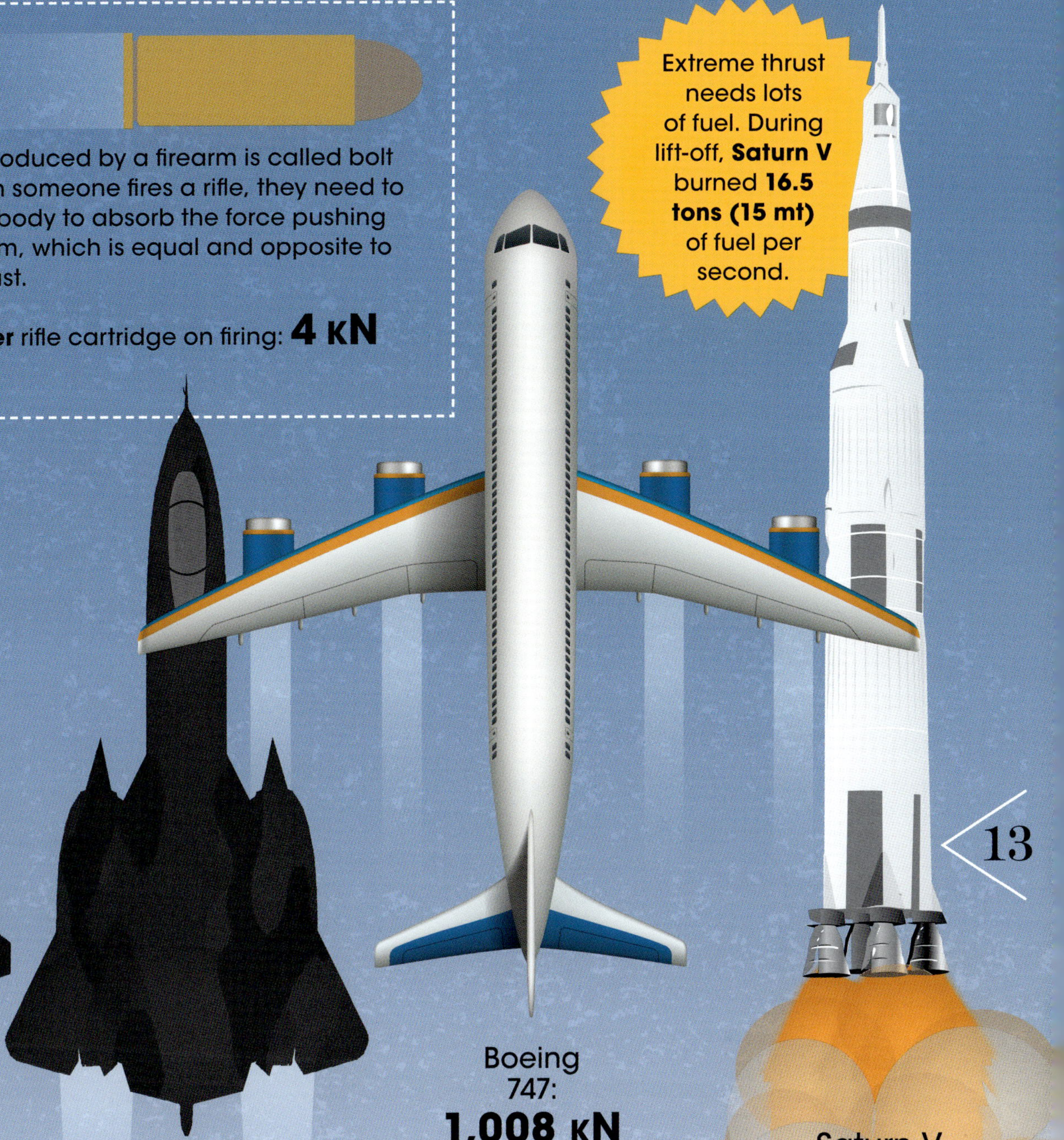

SR-71 Blackbird spy plane: **290 kN**

Boeing 747: **1,008 kN**

Saturn V at launch: **34,500 kN**

Blue whales are some of the strongest animals on Earth. Scientists have discovered that a blue whale with a body mass of about **78 tons (71 mt)** produces about **60 kN** of thrust.

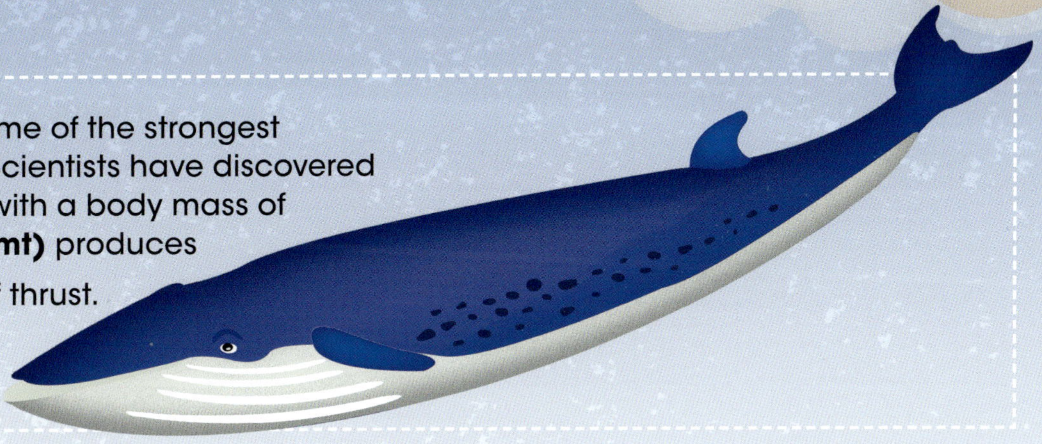

GETTING UP TO SPEED

These super-fast vehicles use rockets, jets, and the power of the sun and the wind to smash speed records on land, sea, through the air, and even in outer space.

SPEED RECORDS

mph = miles per hour
kph = kilometers per hour

LAND

land speed record (any vehicle):
Andy Green, *Thrust SSC7* • 63.035 mph (1227.985 kph)
motorcycle:
Rocky Robinson, *Ack Attack* • 376.36 mph (605.7 kph)
wind-powered:
Glenn Ashby, *Horonuku* • 138.2 mph (222.4 kph)
solar-powered:
Kenjiro Shinozuka, *Sky Ace TIGA* • 56.75 mph (91.332 kph)

Spirit of Australia set the water speed record on **October 8, 1978.**

SPACE

fastest spacecraft:
Parker Space Probe 364,660 mph (586,800 kph)
fastest crewed:
Apollo 10 (lunar mission) 24,791 mph (39,897 kph)
on Mars: Spirit and Opportunity rovers 0.11 mph (0.18 kph)

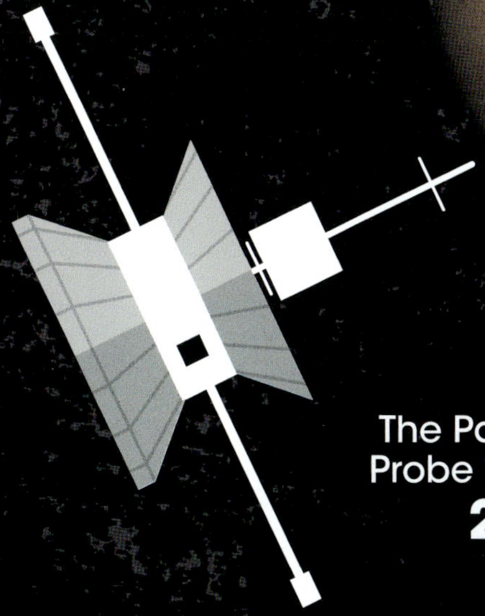

The Parker Space Probe launched in **2018**.

AIR

crewed rocket-powered: William J. Knight, North American X-15A-2 • 4,523 mph (7,270 kph)
crewed jet propelled: Eldon W. Joersz, Lockheed SR-71A Blackbird • 2,081.6 mph (3,350 kph)
helicopter: John Egginton, Westland Lynx 800 • 249 mph (400.87 kph)

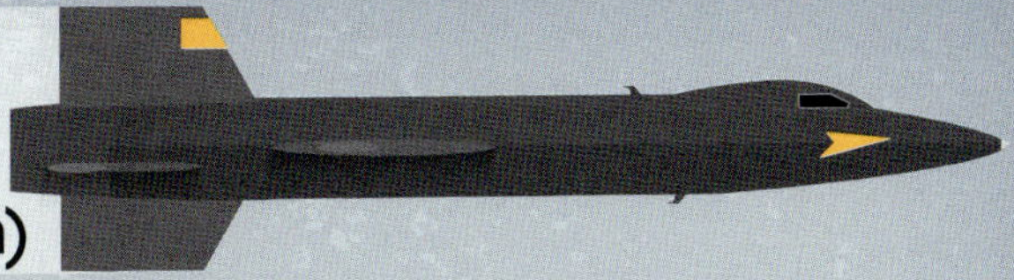

X-15 Hypersonic Aircraft set the Air speed record on **October 3, 1967.**

Thrust SSC7 set the Land Speed record on **October 15, 1997.**

RAIL

maglev (magnetic) train:
SCMaglev L0 • 374.7 mph (603 kph)
wheeled train:
TGV POS V150 • 357 mph (574.8 kph)

SCMaglev L0 set the train speed record on **April 21, 2015.**

WATER

water speed record: Ken Warby, *Spirit of Australia* • 317.58 mph (511 kph)
wind-powered: Paul Larsen, *Vestas Sailrocket* • 75 mph (120 kph)

RUBBING TOGETHER

Friction is the force created when two objects or substances rub past each other. This force works in the opposite direction to motion, making it harder for things to move, but it can have useful effects.

ROUGH AND SMOOTH

- Friction is caused by surfaces rubbing together.
- The rougher the surfaces, the higher the levels of friction.
- To reduce friction, surfaces can be covered in materials called lubricants, such as oil.

BRILLIANT BRAKES

The friction between brake pads and spinning wheels slows vehicles down, but it can produce a lot of heat. The brakes on a Formula 1 car can heat up to 2,192°F (1,200°C) during a race, glowing red-hot when they do so.

BURNOUT

Before they zoom off, super-fast dragsters spin their back wheels to put down a layer of rubber on the track. This increases friction and improves their getaway times.

SUPER SMOOTH

Polytetrafluoroethylene (PTFE) is the long name given to a substance used as a non-stick coating. It's better known as Teflon™. It's used to make non-stick cookware, windshield wipers, protectors for fabrics and carpets, and special coatings to protect machinery in the chemical and steel industries.

HOT RE-ENTRY

Space vehicles coming down to Earth experience high levels of friction as they re-enter Earth's atmosphere. Temperatures can soar to 3,002°F (1,650°C), so they need special heat shields to protect them from being destroyed.

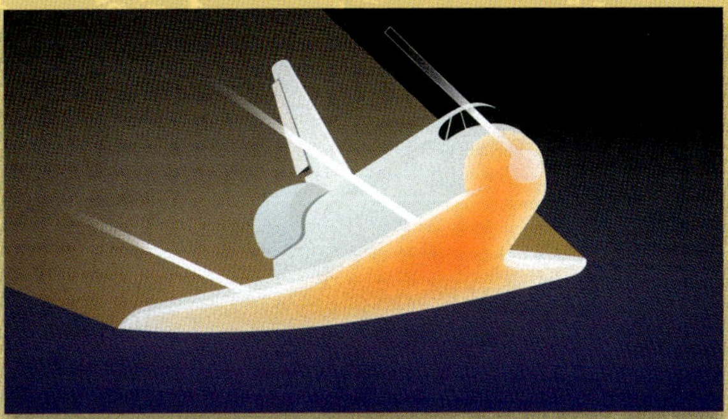

FRICTION STICKS

Stick insects have hairy pads on their legs that increase the friction so much that they can grip branches and hang upside down.

MOVING AT SPEED

In order to move quickly and easily, objects need a streamlined shape that disrupts their surroundings as little as possible as they pass.

WHAT A DRAG!

As an object moves, the substance it passes through, such as air, is disturbed. This disturbance produces a force that acts against the movement, known as air resistance, or drag. The amount of drag an object produces is measured by its drag coefficient. The lower the drag coefficient figure, the more aerodynamic the object.

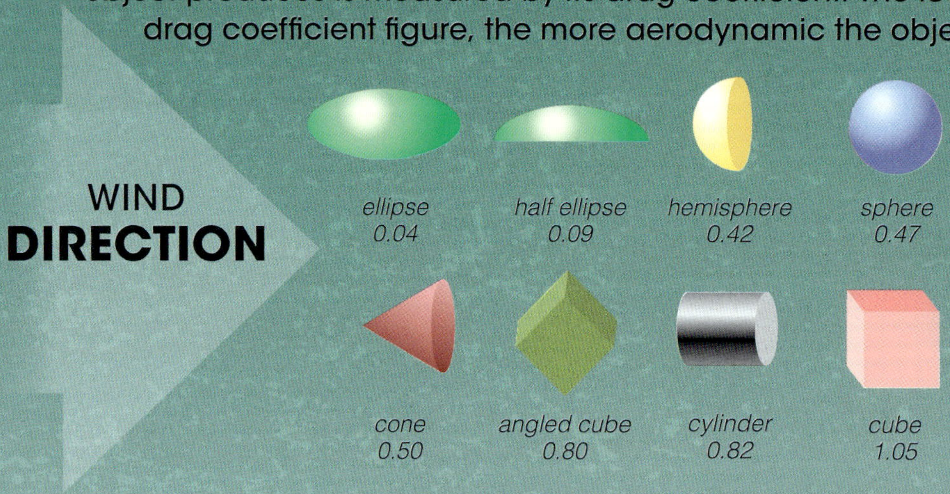

SUPER SWIMMERS

Many animals that live in water have evolved streamlined shapes to give them a very low drag coefficient. This allows them to swim through the water with a minimum of effort.

dolphin in water drag coefficient: **0.0036**

Olympic sprinter: **1.2**

USING AIR RESISTANCE

If you're falling from a great height, then air resistance can be useful. Deploying a parachute increases the air resistance, slowing your rate of fall so you can land safely and in one piece.

ON LAND

Pac-car II is a super-efficient car. Its aerodynamics give it a drag coefficient of **0.075.**

family car: **0.25**

road cyclist: **1.0**

IN THE AIR

Airbus A380........................ 0.0265
small bird 0.4

FEEL THE SQUEEZE

Pressure is a force produced by one object pushing on another. The greater the push, the greater the pressure.

ALTITUDE

At about **50,000 feet (15,000 m)**, atmospheric pressure is about one-tenth that at sea level.

Mount Everest in Nepal is 29,029 feet (8,848 m) high. It is the tallest mountain above sea level.

UNDER PRESSURE

It may not feel like it, but the air is pushing down on you all the time. This is called atmospheric pressure and it changes with altitude (height).

SEA LEVEL

This is the standard used to compare other pressures. The average pressure at sea level is roughly equal to **1 bar** (or 1,000 mb), which is a force equivalent to 100,000 Newtons per square meter.

LOW PRESSURE

At the top of Mount Everest, air pressure is one-third that at sea level. Above about 26,240 feet (8,000 m) is called the "Death Zone" as it's a struggle to survive here without extra oxygen. Water boils at a lower temperature too, and it would take over **18 minutes** to boil an egg.

The deepest SCUBA dive was to more than 1,090 feet (332 m). The pressure is 50 times that at sea level.

ATMOSPHERE

Pressure drops as you move up the atmosphere by about **3.5 mb** for every **100 feet (30 m)**.

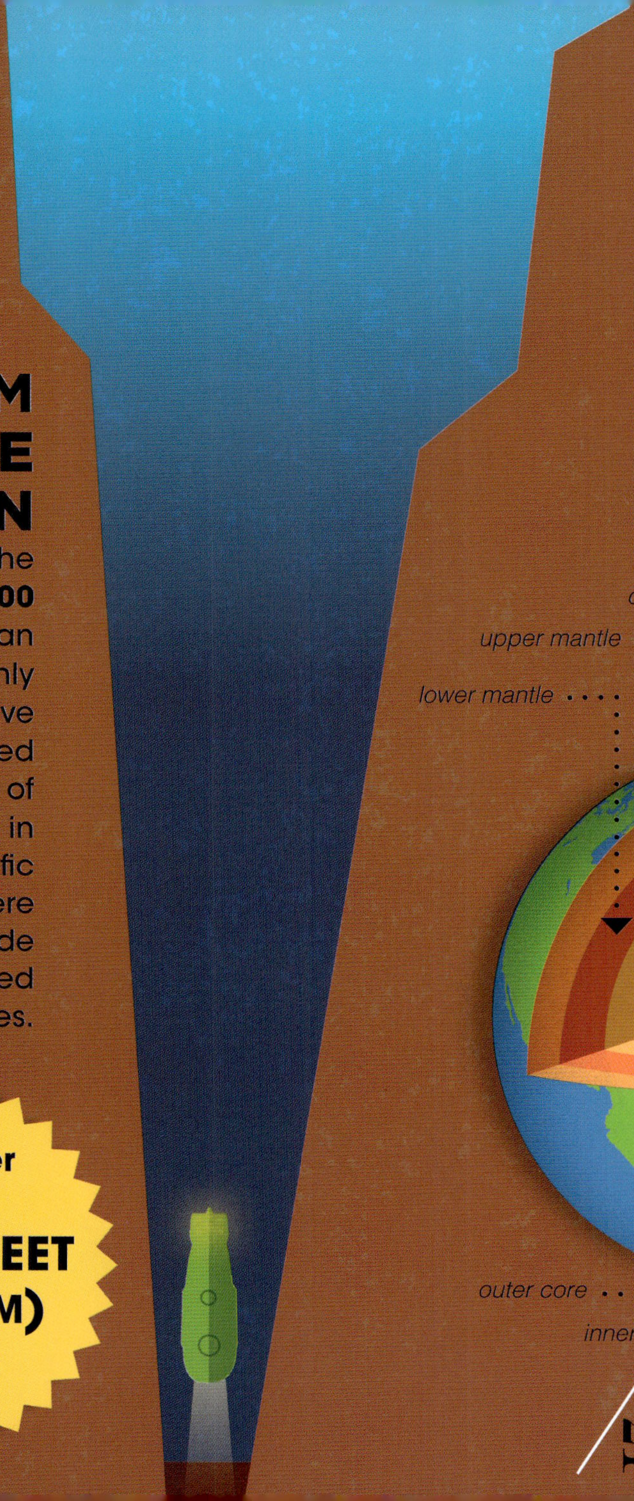

BOTTOM OF THE OCEAN

Down here, the pressure is **1,000** times greater than at sea level. Only three people have ever visited the bottom of Challenger Deep in the western Pacific Ocean. They were safely inside reinforced submersibles.

Challenger Deep is 36,070 FEET (10,994 M) below the surface.

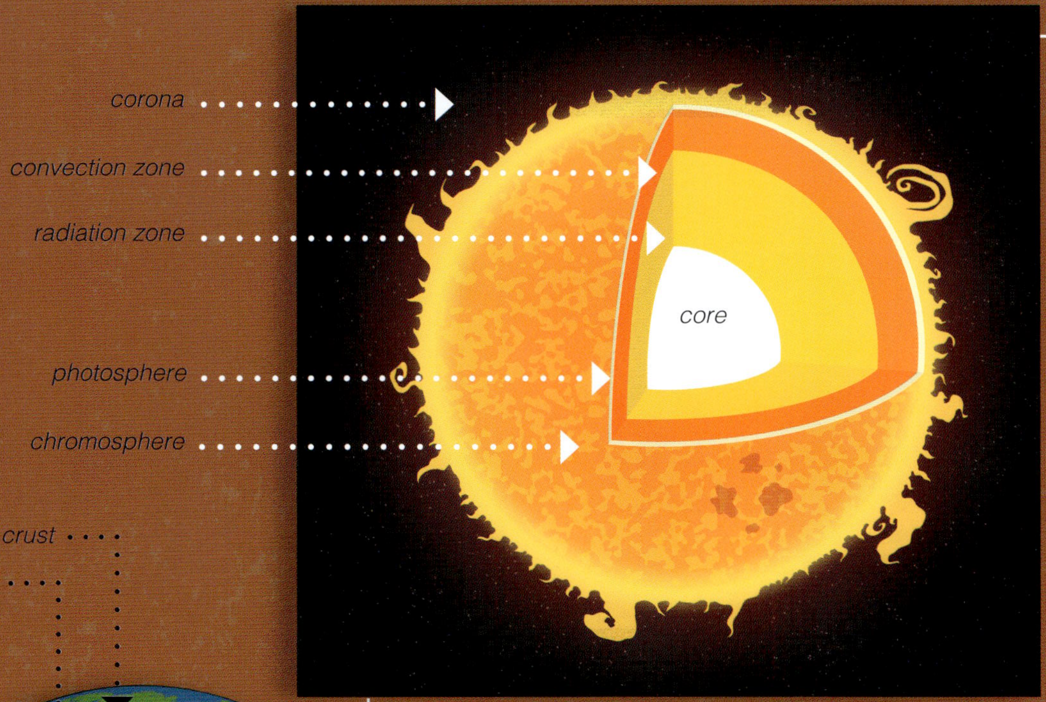

AT THE CENTER OF THE SUN

pressure is **2.477 x 10^{11} bar.** That's **250 billion** times the atmospheric pressure at sea level. That's enough to squeeze atomic nuclei so that they fuse together, releasing the huge amounts of energy that make the sun shine.

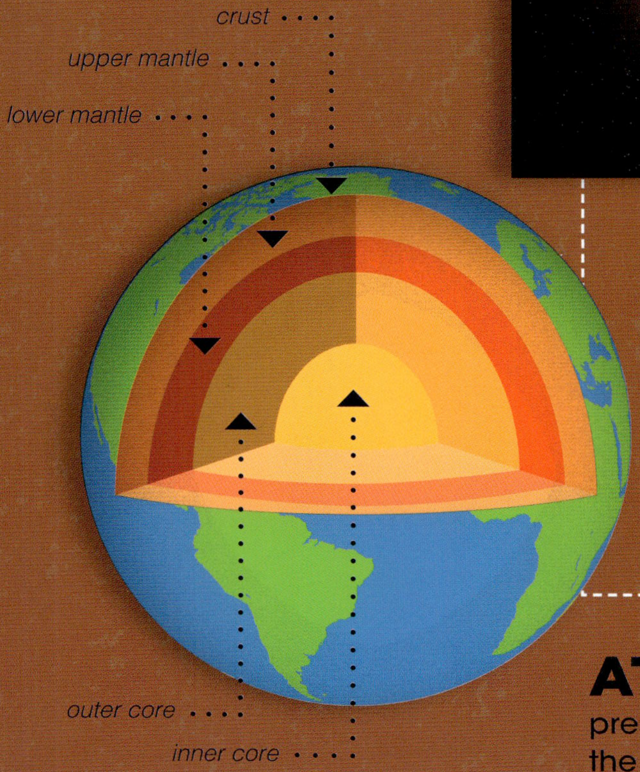

AT EARTH'S CORE

pressure is up to **3.5 million** times the pressure at sea level.

MAGNETIC ATTRACTION

Magnets produce an invisible magnetic field that will attract ferromagnetic materials or push and pull on other magnetic fields. These qualities can be used to power vehicles, help to produce power or study the wonders of the universe.

SUN'S MAGNETISM

Magnetically charged particles move away from the sun's surface in the form of solar wind. The sun's magnetic field is so powerful that its effects are even felt beyond our solar system.

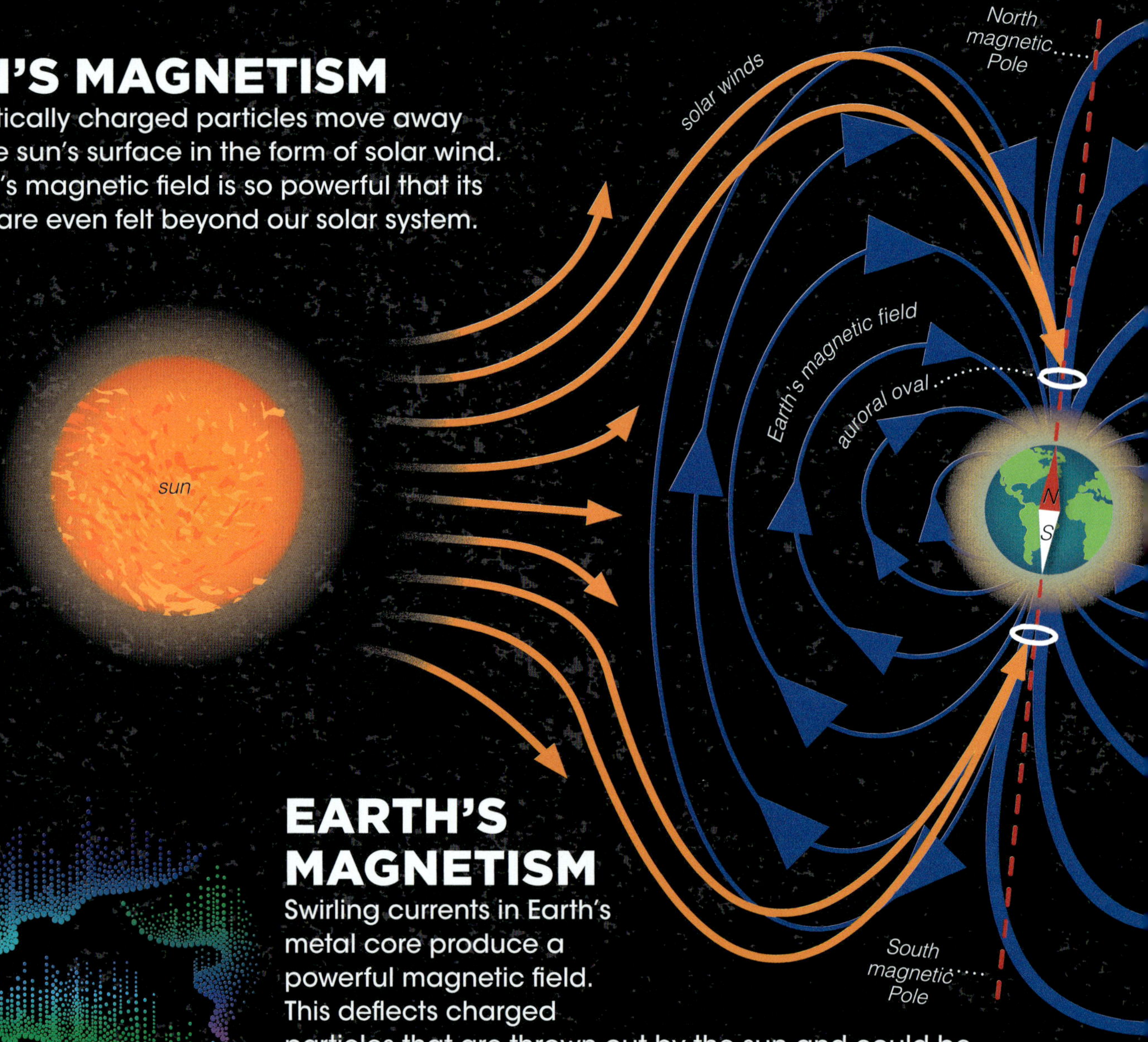

EARTH'S MAGNETISM

Swirling currents in Earth's metal core produce a powerful magnetic field. This deflects charged particles that are thrown out by the sun and could be harmful to living things. Some of the particles are funneled down over Earth's polar regions. Here, they interact with particles in the atmosphere to create the glowing aurorae, spectacular natural light displays in the sky. The regions where this happens are known as the auroral ovals.

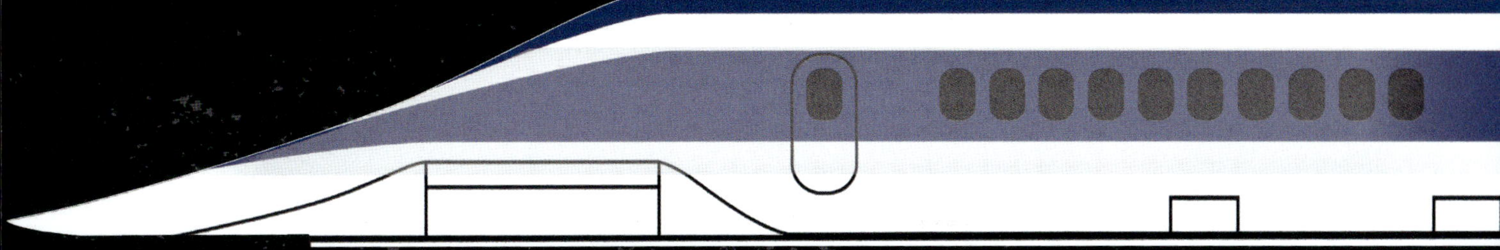

MAGLEV TRAINS

Magnetic forces lift maglev trains above their tracks. Magnets at the front pull on the train while magnets at the back push it. As the trains hover in the air, there is very little friction, allowing them to zoom along at incredible speeds.

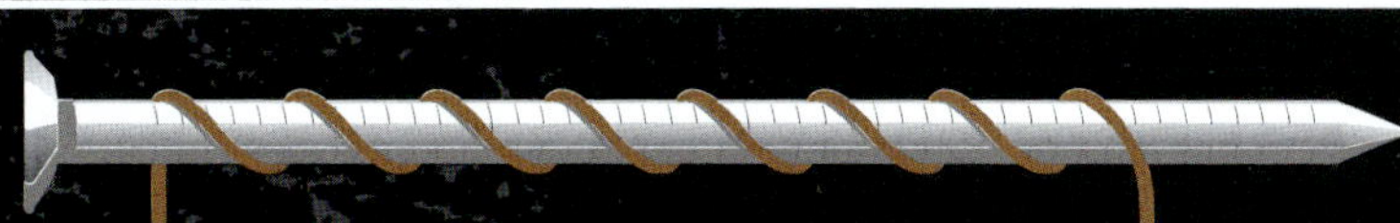

ELECTROMAGNETS

Run an electric current through a wire and it produces a magnetic field. If you wrap this wire tightly in coils it will increase the strength of the field, especially if the wire is wrapped around a metal core.

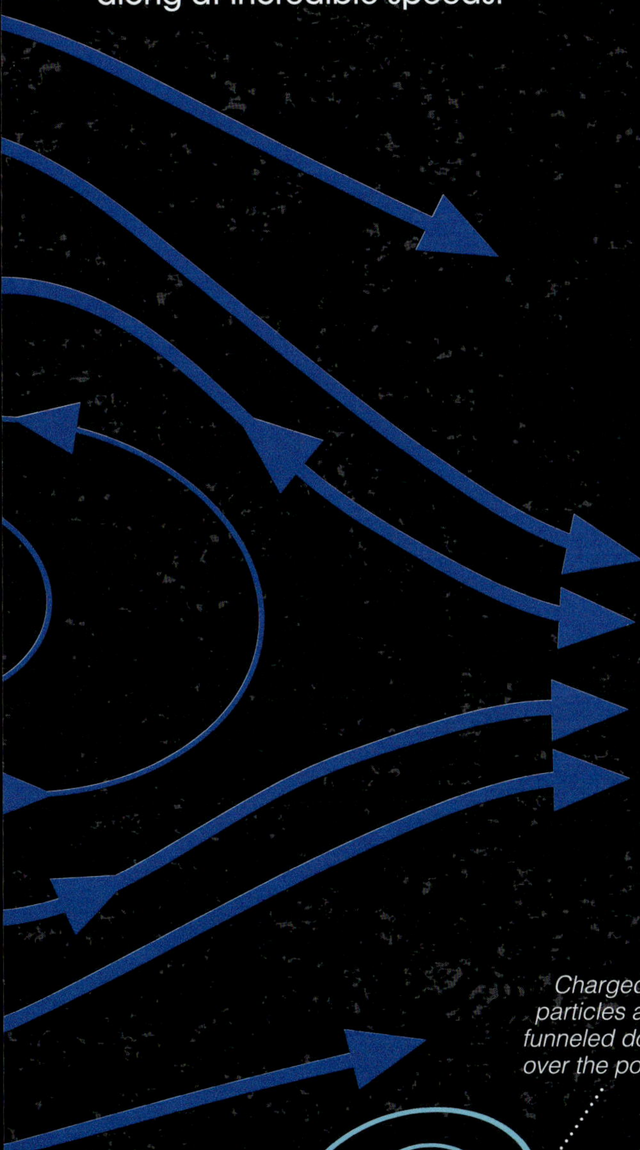

PARTICLE ACCELERATOR

Inside the Large Hadron Collider at CERN on the Swiss/France border, thousands of superconducting magnets produce a magnetic field that's 100,000 more powerful than that of Earth. They are used to keep the beams of particles tight and lined up so that they slam into each other at incredible speed.

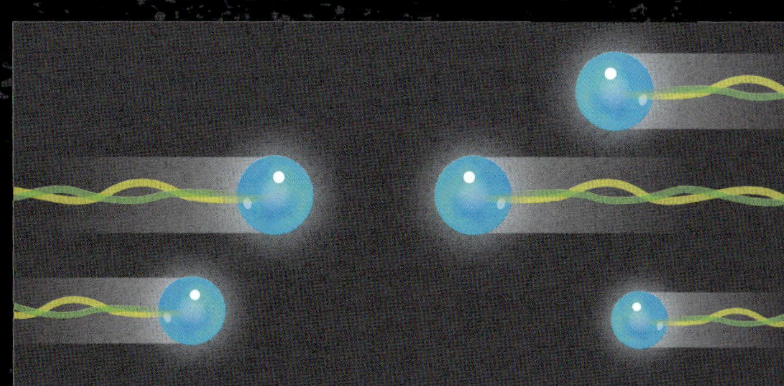

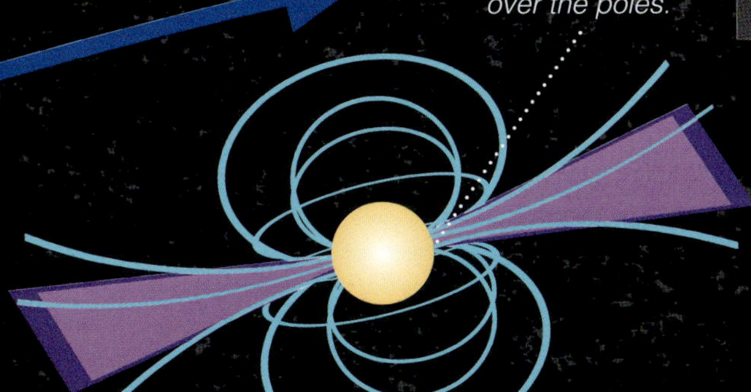

Charged particles are funneled down over the poles.

MAGNETARS

These are the most powerful magnetic objects in the universe. They are magnetic neutron stars and can produce a magnetic field with a strength of **100 billion teslas** (the unit used to measure magnetic fields). In comparison, Earth's magnetic field is only **0.00005 teslas**.

KEEPING THINGS BALANCED

When forces are balanced, then an object's movement (or staying still) remains the same.

SITTING IN A CHAIR

Even when you're sitting still, there are forces acting on you. While you are pushing down on the chair, at the same time, the chair is pushing up with an equal force. These are balanced forces. If the force you pushed down with were greater than that of the chair, then it wouldn't support your weight.

HOT-AIR BALLOONS

Hot-air balloons rise by heating the air inside their envelope (the fabric bag above the basket). Heat makes the air inside less dense than the air outside, causing the balloon to rise. When the upward force matches the force of gravity pulling down on the balloon, then it will stay at the same height.

HELICOPTERS

Helicopters can hover because the lift they produce with their spinning rotors is the same as the force of gravity acting on the helicopter.

MIL MI-26

is the world's largest helicopter. It can weigh up to **61 tons (56 mt)** fully loaded and needs two engines to keep it hovering.

FLOATING SHIPS

When a ship floats, part of it is in the water, while part of it sits out of the water. The part of the ship below the waterline pushes the same volume of water out of the way. The weight of that water is called its displacement. The amount of water displaced weighs the same as the ship and its cargo, so the ship floats.

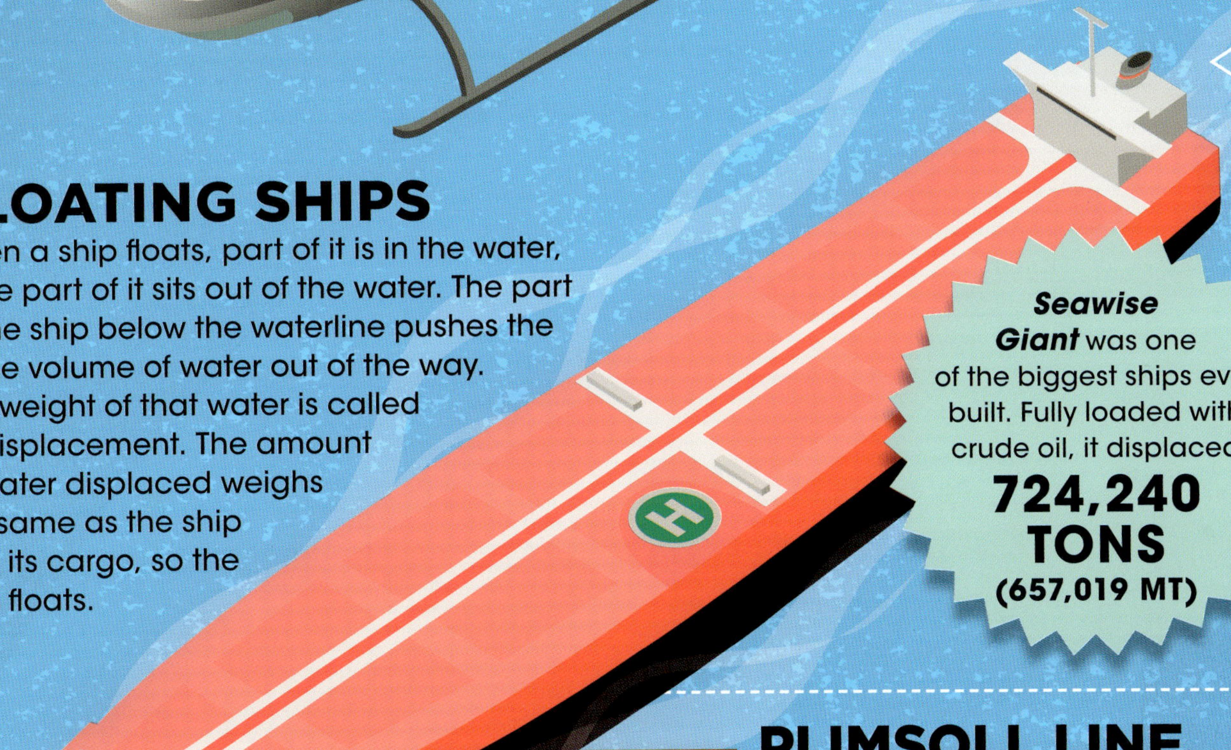

Seawise Giant was one of the biggest ships ever built. Fully loaded with crude oil, it displaced **724,240 TONS (657,019 MT)**

PLIMSOLL LINE

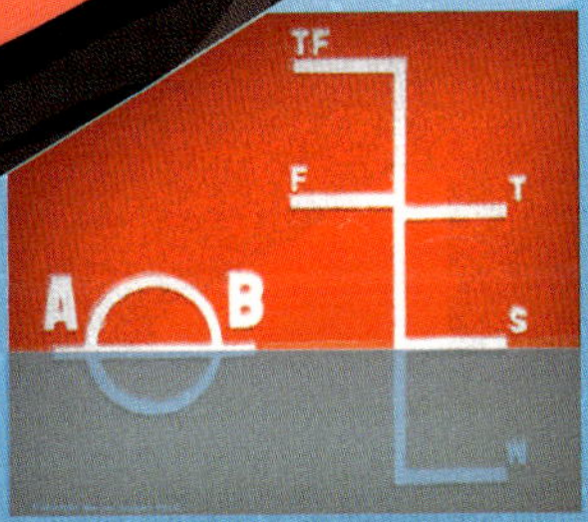

On the sides of all ocean-going ships is a series of lines, called the Plimsoll Line. These show the maximum level that a ship can be loaded to in various weather and water conditions. The heavier the load, the lower the ship will sit in the water.

MASSIVE MACHINES

Machines are designed to make work easier. And if you're digging huge amounts of rock out of the ground, trying to move enormous objects or just building some of the biggest monuments on the planet, then you're going to need some large and powerful machines.

BUILDING THE PYRAMIDS

Ramps are simple machines that make it easier to raise and lower loads. The ancient Egyptians used ramps to help build the pyramids at **Giza** about **4,500 years** ago. The ramps were built up along the sides of the pyramids making it easier to pull the massive stone blocks into place.

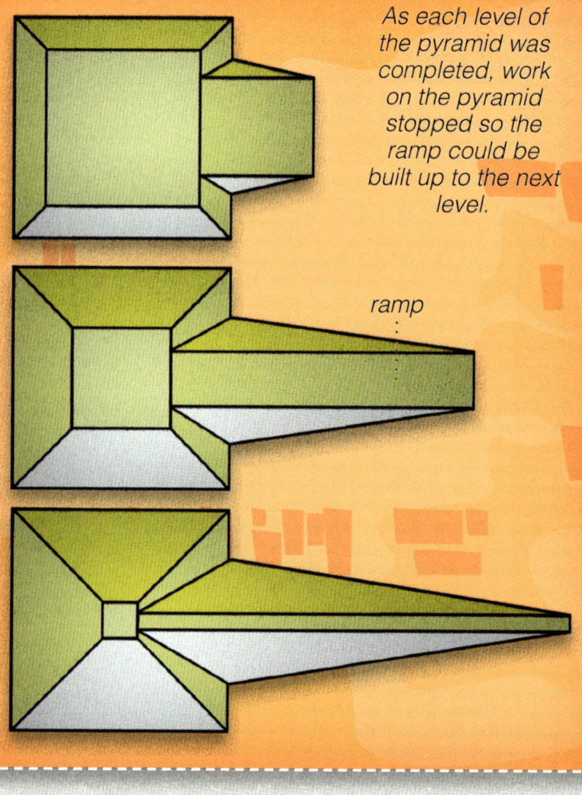

As each level of the pyramid was completed, work on the pyramid stopped so the ramp could be built up to the next level.

BIG DIGGERS

- **Big Muskie**: a dragline excavator with a bucket capacity of **6,003 cubic feet (170 cu m)** (the size of two double-decker buses)
- **The Captain**: a power shovel with a bucket capacity of **4,944 cubic feet (140 cu m)**

BUCKET WHEEL EXCAVATOR

The **Bagger 293** is one of the biggest land vehicles ever built. It can dig up around **242,508 tons (220,000 mt)** of coal every day using its bucket wheel.

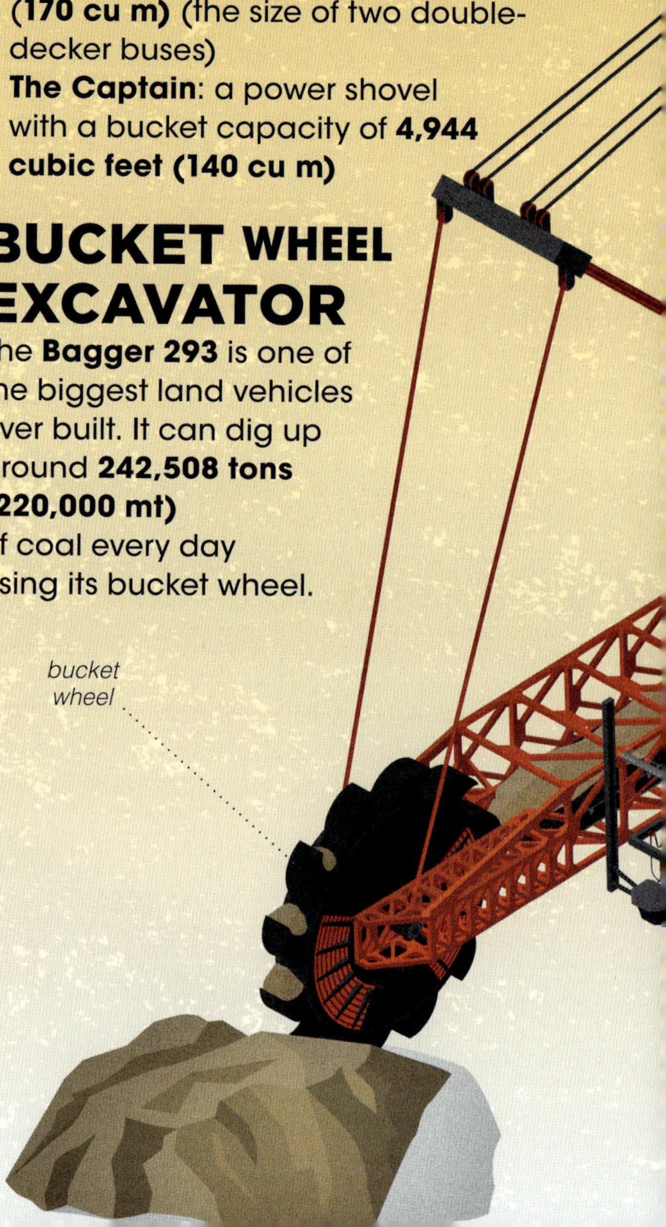

MARION CRAWLER

NASA uses two massive crawler-transporters to move its enormous rockets to the launchpads. The crawlers can carry loads of up to **9,039 tons (8,200 mt)**, and they have been used to move the towering **Saturn V** rockets and the **space shuttles**.

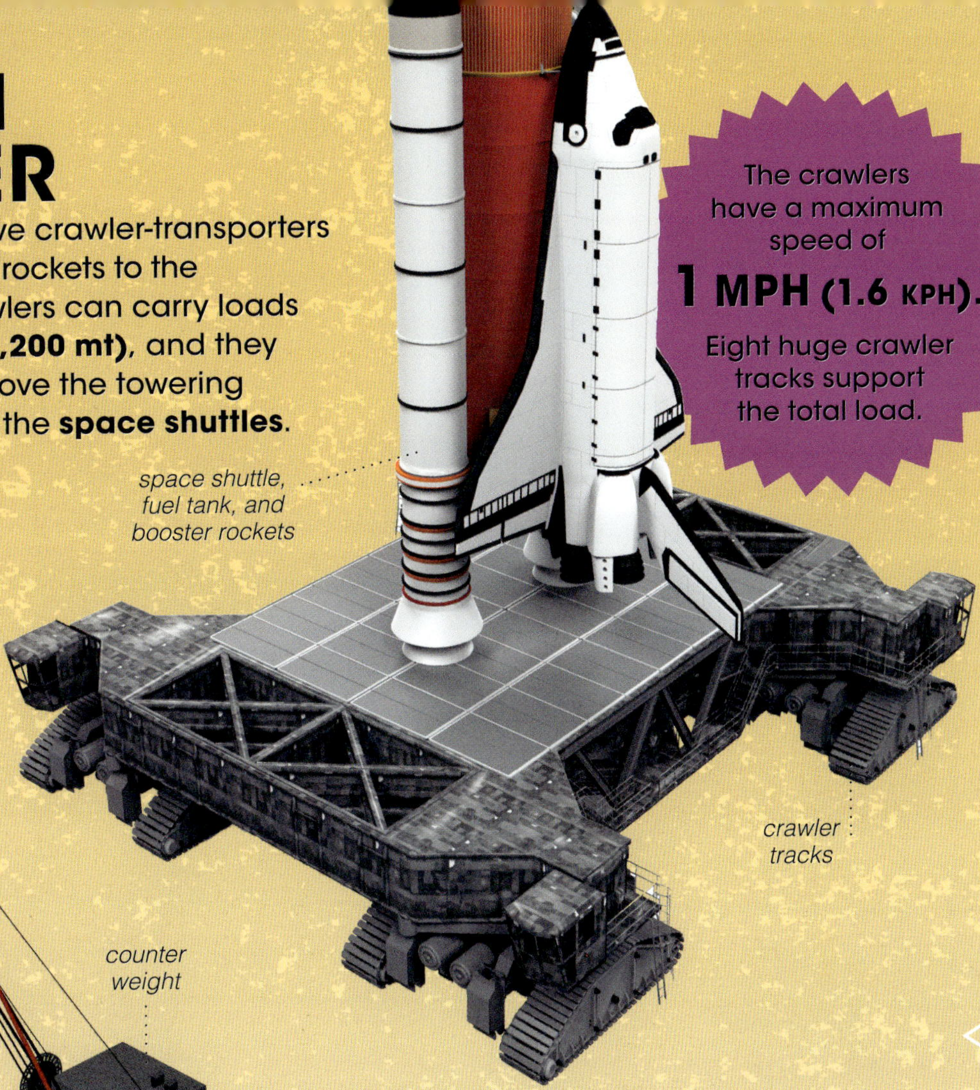

The crawlers have a maximum speed of

1 MPH (1.6 KPH).

Eight huge crawler tracks support the total load.

The Bagger 293's bucket wheel is

70 FEET (21.3 M)

across and has **18 buckets.** Each bucket can hold **530 cubic feet (15 cu m)** of coal.

BIGGEST CRANE

The **Taisun gantry crane** in the Yantai Raffles Shipyard, Shandong Province, China, is used to build ships and oil rigs. It can raise loads weighing up to twice the weight of the Eiffel Tower in Paris, France.

EXTREME ENGINES

Big jobs need big engines and these engines and motors are some of the most powerful on the planet, capable of propeling trains, trucks, cars, planes, and spacecraft to record-breaking performances.

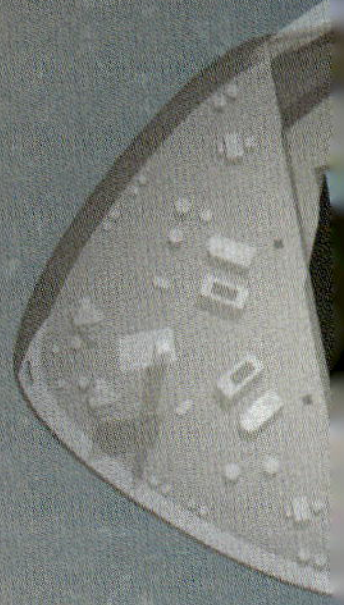

POWERFUL LOCOMOTIVE

Built to move coal throughout China, the HXD1 is one of the most powerful electric locomotives in the world. Its electric motors produce power measuring **19,303 BHP (brake horsepower),** or 14,197 kW (kilowatts).

front view of a jet turbine engine

MOST POWERFUL JET ENGINE

Used on Boeing 747 Jumbo Jets and Boeing 777s, the **GE90-115B** holds the record for the jet engine with the highest thrust ever produced of **513,000 Newtons**.

BIGGEST DIESEL ENGINE

The **Wärtsilä RT-flex96C** engine produces **109,000 BHP (80,080 kW)**, enough to power a small town. It is **44 feet (13.5 m)** tall and weighs nearly **2,315 tons (2,100 mt)**. It is fitted to the *Emma Maersk* container ship.

MOST POWERFUL ROCKET ENGINE

The solid-fuel boosters used to blast the **space shuttle** into orbit produced up to **13,800,000 Newtons** of thrust during lift-off.

This engine will burn through **3,700 GALLONS (14,000 L)** of heavy fuel oil in an hour.

POWERING THE HOUND

- *Bloodhound LSR* is a vehicle designed to smash the land speed record.
- At first, it will be powered by a jet engine. After that, a rocket will take over to blast it to more than **760 mph (1,220 kph)**.

POWERFUL CAR ENGINE

The Bugatti Chiron is fitted with a **8,000 cc** (cubic centimetre) **W16** engine that can produce **1,479 bhp**. In theory, it could push the car to **288 mph (463 kph)** (although the top speed is still unknown!).

The W16 engine is mounted in the middle of the car, giving it a better handling balance.

GLOSSARY

ACCELERATION
A change in the speed or direction of a moving object. When the object is slowing down, this is referred to as negative acceleration.

AERODYNAMIC
Shaped to move easily through air or water with a minimum of friction.

AIR RESISTANCE
A force that acts in the opposite direction to the movement of an object as it moves through air.

ATMOSPHERIC PRESSURE
The pressure caused by the weight of the air in the atmosphere.

ATOMIC NUCLEUS
The small, dense region at the center of an atom. It contains almost all of the atom's mass.

BRAKE HORSEPOWER (BHP)
A measure of the power of an engine. Brake horsepower equals the force that would be needed to counter the engine's power.

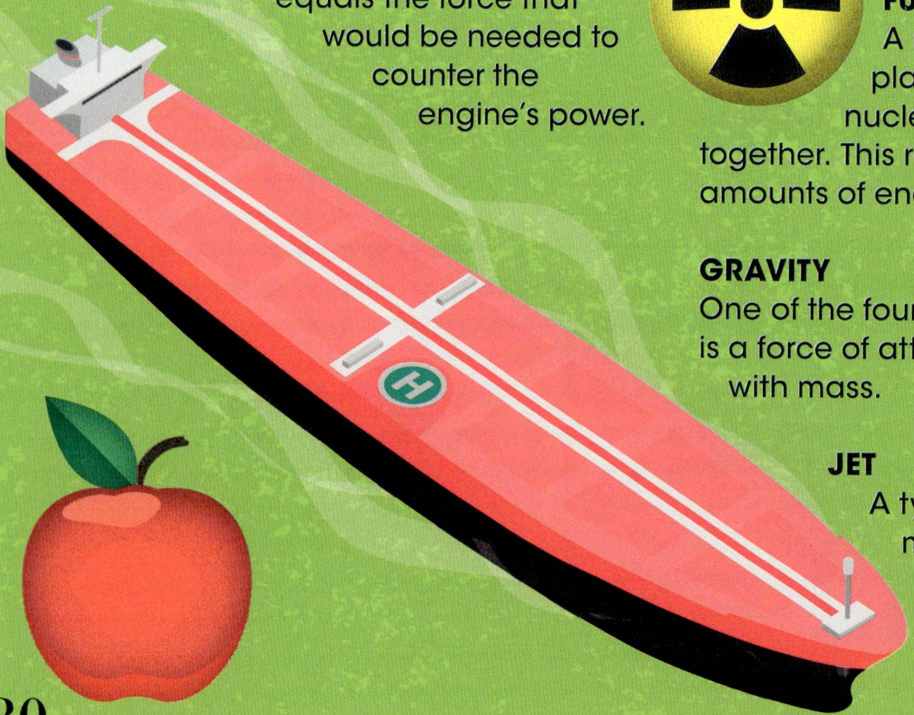

DISPLACEMENT
The volume occupied by the submerged part of a ship that would otherwise be occupied by water.

DRAG
A force that acts against the direction of movement as an object moves through air or water. Air resistance is a form of drag.

ELECTROMAGNET
A magnet that is created by passing an electric current through a wire wrapped around a metal core.

ELECTROMAGNETISM
One of the four fundamental forces. Electromagnetism holds atoms together, and also produces light. It is produced by an interaction between electrically charged particles.

FRICTION
A force created when two objects rub against each other, slowing down movement.

FUSION
A nuclear reaction that takes place inside stars, in which the nuclei of atoms are squeezed together. This reaction releases huge amounts of energy and makes stars shine.

GRAVITY
One of the four fundamental forces, gravity is a force of attraction between objects with mass.

JET
A type of engine that burns a mixture of fuel and air to produce hot gases. The gases roar out of the back of the jet, pushing the vehicle forward.

LIFT
A force that acts on a moving body in an upward direction. As an airplane moves forward, the air passing around its wings produces lift.

MAGLEV
Short for "magnetic levitation," a kind of train that is powered by magnetism.

MAGNET
An object that can pull certain kinds of materials toward it using the force of magnetism. A magnet has a north and a south pole. Fields of magnetic force run between the poles.

MASS
The amount of matter that an object contains.

PRESSURE
A measure of the amount of force being applied to an object per unit of area.

PROTON
A particle with positive electrical charge, found inside atoms.

STRONG NUCLEAR FORCE
One of the four fundamental forces of nature, the strong nuclear force holds together the particles inside an atom.

SUPERCONDUCTOR
A material that conducts electricity with no resistance when cooled to very low temperatures. Maglev trains use electromagnets made from superconducting wires.

THRUST
A force that drives a vehicle forward. Thrust is produced by a jet engine by forcing out hot gases in one direction. This produces an equal and opposite reaction that moves the vehicle in the opposite direction.

WEAK NUCLEAR FORCE
One of the four fundamental forces of nature, the weak nuclear force makes possible the nuclear reactions that power the sun.

WEIGHT
A measure of the force exerted on a body by gravity. The more mass the object has, the greater its weight.

INDEX